IT LOOKS LIKE A MAN

A Wesleyan Chapbook

IT LOOKS LIKE A MAN

Poems by
Heather McHugh

:::

Wesleyan University Press
Middletown, Connecticut

Wesleyan University Press
Middletown, Connecticut 06459
www.wesleyan.edu/wespress

ISBN 978-0-8195-0240-7

Front and back cover photographs
courtesy of the author.

CONTENTS

CONTENTS

Acknowledgments

IT LOOKS LIKE A MAN

WE TRY TO SPEAK EACH OTHER'S TONGUES

The girl was blinded in a glance; the guy was
high on weed but understood

the elder in his cups. The guzzler
graduated down the spectrum

to a sip. No one appeared too far away because
a mirror in a corner of the room

could bevel every wow. The sky began to bring
a star-scape up, and suddenly

a midnight sharpened every gleam. The byte
is eight bits long. You touch

those buttons, said the hooker, and you'll see
how much a lowland holds. Yes, that;

your mountaintop can fit. (My flattery, your
puffery, were never opposites.)

THE ONLY STAND-OUT AT THE DANCE

I cannot take your time. I'm out of step.
I'm going with a flow but not the flow.
My periods are not the data-entry points
of any self-respecting pedagogue. Duh
problem is duh part dat's

mentalized: The cartoon cat gone splat
when leaping to a cartoon dog's
conclusions. You see I cannot stem
my surges, stalk the proper prey.
Excuse me. I have got to paint

this railroad tunnel on
this wall, before
my followers can
get away.

TWO WIDOWS, MAKING A BED

Look at this! What a wonder to find it here,
under the covers, and out of its box.
It's equipped for some duty, to judge
by its crankshaft. The structure's
a beauty. I bet that it walks.

Turn it on! Can you find any
switch for ignition? They haven't designed many
I'd like to keep. It should rise, it should shine,
it should take a position! (Not
kill our ambition or put us to sleep.)

Does it sit? Can it stand? It has spin, it has spyware.
Its handles aren't mangled, so why does it lie there?
With stir-stick and fur-trick, a can that's a zinger,
it looks like a man.
But it won't lift a finger.

I guess it's a protoype—check that
display, neither coming to senses, nor going away!
If it's this hard to start it, we never
could pause it. Just give me a hand.
It can go in the closet.

RULEBOOK FULL OF ERGOS

Do not scratch the dog's letter.
He's going to share the bed.

Do not nullify the nun
however heavily invested.

Notwithstanding elephants in every room
we loved our share of ass.

But soon the boots began
to get that spat-up shine.

How long before we all incline
to heels? That all depends. On what? On gravity.

The high life has its lowlife: jerks are coming
to infect us with some

national neurology. Some corpuscles won't hang with
anyone who doesn't look like them (God knows

they look suspect.) You see
I use the royal We, myself.

Abuse is what we mean by use.
So Amos, Mon

Amour, we have to keep
our sneakers handy.

DISPUTE WITH MANIFESTI

Luther never mollified an Eve. Lord, give her
luthiers instead. It takes too many syllables to nail
the best intentions to the bedroom door.

It's better hearten than harangue your forces.
Give me dashing gigolos or journalists:
They understand the bangs, and curve the cantos,

sharpen shivers. Let the light
hit home. The nuns who taught us
English, calling our ellipses

just "suspended periods"
had underestimated what was intimated
when they made a sacrament of someone's

moniker; that's how the Word became
some bloody gift of God to
You-Know-Who. To What's-His-Name.

I WANT ONE OF MY OWN

How could it feel?
With every inch? It's just

so gorgeous an engorgement—or,
more delicately put,

emerging gentry. From go it makes
a straight-up invitation to the contra-dichter.

Temporary sceptre, say, endowed
with coddlability and doublability and more—

it's worth the extra
lip service and rubberwork

when you behold it
purpled to the hilt:

an object for the shaking
maybe with amusement

in a flash of higher purpose, or for-
saking, in a depth of underground.

Come on now, sis, let's take a nip
while we still can. (Its own

manhandler, soon enough,
is coming round.)

∴∴

X's FROM YOUR ONLINE POETRY GENERATOR

"Publishing your poem will stop it changing."

No shit, Sherlock.
If you did it for the carrot
think again: a writer's never fed.
Dessert is not forthcoming, so you'll get

the stick instead.
Instead is not a repetition trigger
like again. But don't let that
disturb your programming.

Three candymen ago I was
a whippersnapper like yourself. And look
what happened next: A miss, a miz,
associate professor—then

the full-time bore. (Ago's
a repetition trigger.) You may love
the shortness of the stick,
I get it. But watch out, with all that

twisted foil around, you risk
addiction to the glitter on the smack.
You'll crave a thousand X's or a million M&M's
from MMXX onward and towards

transcalculi of ken. Ai! Ai!
Or so Cassandra warned.
She cried in tongues! But when
Tech Services arrived

to quiet her and all her semblances, they
automated everything. With well-oiled kissers
they could whisper things. Like shh.
And shhh. And shhhh again.

.

THEY LEFT IT TO BEAVER

So the streams got clogged. That didn't stop the global wars, the arts
of governance, the stars revising lines of fashion and deploying new
attention spans. (Where once great uncles could anticipate the Pearly
Gates, the lesser settled for the Golden, then a generation later we

broke Water.) In time, the Times was set aside
for news, with funnies just to keep the kiddos tuned.
The screens went port and starboard, huge. The TV Guide
was suddenly on the TV, and had a channel number.

Welcome to the meta-century. We made our livings with our lives,
and we believed in fencing off the hazmats when we reassigned
outdated forts. The Indians were moved away
from every island that had once

been named for them. Our local one
became an ammo dump. Fort Knox
got hard and harder currencies, the kind
we soon enough desire to call defunct. As for

Fort Worth, after Ornette, who knows? I know (from signs devised
by the departments of interior) Fort Worden's history
has led to poets and musicians. And you wonder why
the country voted for no-nonsense! Nowadays

too few of us recall what real surprises were
(they were inside your Cracker Jacks), or what
Good Humor meant, or how a doctor once
so profited from quints. And none of us

foresaw how fast the multitudes
would all come bursting out:
This buncha babies, born to be
opinionated electronically—

and all called Boomer.

.

SUGAR CHEMISTRY AND PORN

You came out hooked on meaning, then decided
you were born for it. You saw

amino acids in the sky and called them chemtrails. Nature's way too
tolerant of our mistakes, much less

of our successes. Someone's lovely child arrives and we can't help
ourselves: such eye-lights and elaborated hallways

to her wiring and her plumbing!
Wow! Could such a luck be ours?

Those neurosensitivities in filigree, her fingertips,
the crystals of her sugar chemistries! Her likes

could kill a man, once his desire has dipped
its ladle in too many cellars

of saliva, or has lavished
half a lifetime on the soft-serve line. What might

you want, a hot-fudge heart attack? To turn her in
to your own private *raison d'être*? Meanings being

heaped upon the means, the mind
begins to imitate the hive. It puts

some stingers on its wand, and thinks
to weaponize a fondle. Look alive.

MOON SHOT

How did the man go over? Trippingly? Nobody laughed
when he was wittiest, nor loved him best when he
was acting saintly. Still, the fall

is fascinating. And in view of what will come, we need
the patches of forgivability in circumstance, the mini-
series miseries, the common stages of our many

humankinds. A world's a work, just in and of itself.
The winding, winded kind of wit. A hill wept into
shape, with ha-has stitching down its sides

to blind the animals. (They think it's just another
fence, tricked out in ribs and sob-stabs.) So many
forms to be misunderstood, so much to parse

apart, like anima from animus. I couldn't
for the life of me imagine how a soul,
once snagged, has ever gotten over it.

(Perhaps we never cease to be
that disappointed child, the one that,
in his wisdom, Rover bit.)

NIHIL PRIVATIVUM IN THE HOUSE OF KEN

Every night the etymologist is caring for his wife,
but what we mean by care keeps changing. Alzheimer's:
Not so *heimlich*. (Sometimes old and often shady

only mean gone sun.) For eyes and hair, read
looks and strokes. She had the blinkable, the tossable. But Ken
could never breathe for all the kissing.

Now lust is lost. He isn't un-depressed, himself. (Is that
a double or a triple negative? One of the realler nothings, or
just something missing?) Definition doesn't do away

with ends, for all your etymology. Point out
the bone across the room with your own
forefinger and There! the dog comes willingly

to lick your index. Many years, he's tried
to translate your whole handbook, he who once upon a time
could tell so many things together—

and apart, by simple touch of nose. So now
he's thinking "Humans! Stuck in their own
literals! They'll die from either

either/or, or else
from both. Too little or too much."
Thus Fido's mind begins to grind

the beans. Wake up and smell!
Despite my years of effort, he decides,
this poet never meant too well.

LIFE: THE FILM

Language throughout.

:::

BY YOUR LEAVE

At first it was rookeries hooked me.
Then turtles, those bumps on a half-submerged log.
And the mirrors are dabbled by stirrers, so one
turns to two. Where are you in these

parklands of oak and arbutus? A star-entwined arbor
stands guard over art. (Art's a woman of granite,
engraved in the rain of the evergreen
needles.) One's never alone.

Near the pool where the willows all
wallow in wavery lines, overseen by no less
than a moon, which is full, as its lovers require
of their kin, we are duly

in love with our figures, of course.
Man o man! Make me well, with your shades
and your shine. For a flash
make me good.

For a night make me mine.

MOVE 37

The uttermost is a figment of addiction, like
the pre and post we think we deepen takes
or leapen data with. And zounds!

the charge fulfilled, a mount to
measure—all hands up!—I give
some tiny overcrop to every moon.

Or call it newer, older, golder, blue.
The freedom to say all becomes
the blur of seeing sound aligned, unwise,

with our two turns of mind
who for the life of us could never bear the being
clapped or even just yclept

in bounds.

MAYBE IT'S NOW

Maybe it's now
Where the past falls away.
Where we can't find the time
For adoring today.

Was the decade sublime
That a moment could kill?
Was our passionate climb
Only over the hill?

Would your fondest reprieve
Come the moment you'd leave?
Then I'd miss you, and how.
But then maybe it's now?

*

Is our evermore over?
Our dreamtime all done?
Was it only a nevermore
Rising at dawn?

Must the heart be downcast
After one honeymoon?
Can a love never last
To the end of the tune?

Maybe no. Maybe Chronos
Would never allow.
Maybe never is imminent.
Maybe it's now.

*

Could you stand by me fast?
Can we howl for the moon
Not to keep flying past?
Could we love while we burned

Or refrain while in tune?
Maybe Chronos, who knows us,
Will chance to allow
One eternity extra.

Let's make it now.

WOMAN ON THE CLIFF

The fleeting human cannot help her
staking claims, inscribing stones
at all the utmost outposts—headlands
against straits the sunken boat called dire.
One point is fastest still, there at

its implicated anchor. In a moment's ultimatum
solitude seeks out the undivided
or unlettered view, some way to look,
past fix or focus, past taxonomies
of kind, past mind's inclining to make less of one,

or more of everything. She'd hoped to see
her way around, or through. But no. No
foothold on the lapidary slip, where rocks are turning
into verbs, and verbs are nature's answer to a name
like Desolation Point. All subdividing sprays

become suggestive of the companies
nobody can withstand,
except to standing's detriment. The mental world's
a monolith, I grant you that. But matter
is a work of sand.

DOWNEAST YELLOWCAKE AND CHEESEBALLS

We gave the representative a big red button
that his government could use for just
resetting our relations.
Chiefly uncles.

Six feet down, from North
Duquesne to the Ukraine,
great-aunts were spinning.
We had much to learn

from Google maps in Washington, the city
not the state. We thought of time and space
as ours, above all. North is up. When I say We
I do mean Me, but that would change

the case. I care too much
in any of the cases. When I say number
it's comparative, like government
without the fuss. When I say ME,

I do mean US. A general is just
below a president. But barely!
Thumbs have been bestowed for
ups and downs. A big red button is a must.

MIGHTY LOW

the largesse of the sea is well-nigh
unimaginable—spreading wings
to give us onlookers

a slender inkling of
the wealth in just one purse-seine
one quick clutch

of which the snap is never quite
sufficiently enclosing nor
are other kinds

of grasping liable to give
the shrimp farm of our self-
aggrandizement so much as

an inkling of the scale
a scientist acquires
from feel for tail

in full recoil
around a zygote's
version of attachment

BEFORE AND AFTER

What you can't take
with you as
it happens

you will settle for
in just the eyeblink of your
photo-finish

as if comprehensive
solitude could make up for
those losing loves in which

you found yourself
at times as
prodded by superlatives

as plumped by sums

PAST HIM

That's where
I wouldn't put it—past him
say, or even

as a question put it
right before him—would not
smack of need or breathe

of ultimates—so he could
give himself the necessary
props to keep

his spirits up and praise
the woodpile of
his name—lest being

called a mighty oak
the perfect kindler's kept
from catching flame

∴

CONTENTS

1. FLUTE

I was trying to find the thread they said no
one should lose but (man!) she looked so
soft, a force-field gotten up in bedclothes as
the world was snowing
items: news we were to take
for presents, right on up
until it was too hard
to pick her out from drifts.

2. JEROBOAM

Whether you incline
to call it up or short
depends on what you see
as time—as more and more of it
is made for filling
mouths or the exact
expensive taste in
tongues and choppers.

3. MAGNUM

Honkytonks were grinding out their
lengths of wave in geomorphic strips wherever Groovin'
was requested there two centuries could pour
from every second split yet dancing nude
she couldn't touch herself (need we say more)
no zoning law allows for feelings to ensue
once county chest-beaters have been
appropriately vested.

NATIONAL PLACE SETTINGS

A stick or two can do it all.
Can fatten up a fire or stir
varieties of rice to

solidarity. It's naturally made
to order, noun or verb,
an app to feed

a countlessness entire.
But hey, put down your dukes
of righteousness. I'll say

the fork is brilliant, too—
with several stabs
at subdivision, all its lines

distinguished to impress
the stuff of mere totality
with teeth. It makes

of marks its own remarks,
of nouns its own renown.
It multiplies the monolith. By nature

it brings numbers
to desire. (But also this:
a tininess.)

MEANING, TO AND FRO

Your faith in will will need
some chiropractics, for the
auto-accidents; your faith in point of view

some ophthalmology. You master me but I can only
miss you. See? That transitive
will not compute. Our gist

is vertical, a wordy rudder thanks to which
the bloodshot whole horizon gets
subsected. Taste (which used to run

to writ) was dawned on.
Not for good. Only in brainpans.
Sometimes one is

plied, and sometimes
multiplied. Light of my eye,
my appleworks, remember mayors

muster posses
that can run our little mob around
as well as our collective will has done. The dark

of outlook and the light of insight
wind up marrying, but must we raise so many
kinds of glass

to clarify our misery? I mean,
our mastery. God help me, or Roget, that's not
quite it! The word is mystery.

JOKE HEART

The lungs laughed.
The calipers whispered.
The gout having caught on
Musils had to mease. The hands

Forgot, so the head
Took drumming lessons.
Drumming lessens
The length of the joke.

∴

GIST

The pure-bred Pakistani has another spanakopeta and tells
the South Korean engineer a little story. Since she was born in 1982
she has preferred to be addressed as Beth. And then when she was taken
for a woman there were consequences, one of which, a boy,
she gave up to the old-zeal relatives.

The other one, a daughter, she could bring up
European, as she wished. And now he's naturalized.
How do you mean, inquires the man from Nice. (He sounds
a little Macedonian to me.) The conversation gets, let's say,

a *soupçon* tense. Perhaps it is the future. Quite despite its name,
a quiet skylit pine is standing up for happy sappy times. Remember how
that one guy said I ought to come more quietly, because his ex was right

next door? The dog has now induced in the Norwegian visitor
a bout of asthma. Double Stolis get her over it,

thank God (forgive the word).

I feel responsible, of course. I am
the host, supposed to keep

the drinks, but not the feelings,
mixed. I never boast
of having been descended,

like a thought, straight down from two
reputed testicles, or up from one
anteriority of queen. This night, of all the nights,
when representatives of every earthly

pride and stripe are gathered
in the name of a soirée, I find myself
abruptly swearing (by my only stole and negligée)
my fealty to Mort, my old Amor, instead of any lesser
posthumousnesses the adulterated woman ought to woo.

A TOAST TO WILLIAM GASS

Of wild excess he made a palpable necessity.
Such wicked Englishes as his
could turn a ton of Aristotle to a lick
of trill, our hopes of human tryst
to histories of trope. The man was one mean
logophile. (A reader loves

a writer's loving words.) So here's a glass
to William Gass, whose *Fiction and the Figures of Life*
so handily becomes *The Unofficial Deist Offering.*
And lord, how lovely is *On Being Blue,* that
One Gun Bible—wizard words

to whisk us eggheads up, while keeping big ideas
congenial. Given such a skeptical
intelligence, could we not keep his wits aglee
about our own departments of philosophy?

He knew how much "more harm than good"
a human claim of goodness stands to do. And all the while
(past mere repute) he played the living daylights from
a lute! My God, no wonder William Gass is

paramount on my Parnassus. Let's raise another glass to such
a legacy! I call for tropes, for telescopes!
At literary heaven's door
there are so many comers and so few arrivers,
just to build a high enough salute I'd need

another seven screwdrivers.

FAM, FEMME, FAME, FAIM, FIN

for Rich Hladky

Words with wedges, sledges having slips,
The bow, the bough, madrona known

By names you cannot tell apart
From its own motherlands, the flesh

It once was spoken in. Remember
How its naked wood would shine,

The hinter? Just to show
The way to love! You throw

Your books of shade at it, and still
It will not splinter.

FOREVER IS NOT MERCIFUL

Taken from the stand-point, serious,
Of earth, the sky is scary.
It is where a man could fall

Forever, if forever were
A self-respecting term.
The sky is scary and the heart

goes catapulting past. Is God up there
With something, so to speak,
In hand? Protractor? Maybe con-?

What would you say
To such a god? "How do
You do?" What answer would

You settle for? "I'm not
Too bad"? In popular
Democracies, a god had better

Understand unruly
Ways of life, giving a shit,
Giving a fuck, learning to live it

Down. Not up.

BOOM! THE PRESENT

Take it back. I cannot bear the box of words, these
essays made of English sentences, however they
may claim to serve. This wasn't what I meant

by endlessness, this made-up kind of mind, this
mock edition called complete.
The kids could count

on countlessness to keep them company, it was
expected. They would go on having
grandkids, play their cards

more dreamily than we. But some
among the women always did
refuse the sentimental parts,

the olden golden ones, the permanent and period
to which we once were all
consigned. Some humans leap

beyond their place in time, their pre-ordained
allotments (in penultimates and letterforms), their price
in seizures at the heart, to pay

homage to something myriad:
the unforeseeable, the un-foreclosable.
And now we have a hundred

upper cases, with their disambiguations.
Can there be a heaven past The Cloud?
No matter how you ask for more,

it comes out more-or-less. I didn't know
how old the news would get. I dreamt of rock at twelve,
at forty-two of glasses, and throughout my second seventies

in streams of sand. I said I lived for love,
but I was wary of the high command. Eventually
eventfulness ran out. And I—

who'd fled from family, and found
the perfect death doula at last, a gnomish elf—
I still remember where my forebears

kept The Book of Life.
They kept it well above
The Book of Knowledge shelf.

:::

AT LAST

Suppose you let them bring you
round, and hope to entertain you
with TV again, when all you really wanted

was the right IV, to die
without more researches into the relative
degrees of suffering. Suppose

you could not bear more views, reviews;
more prelates, post-its, postulates;
or any second onlyness to come: Would all

the pudiations then
be doubled down? The licenses be voked?
Betrothals nounced? In time will all things

turn out right? Or worse? Which moral code
will levy heavier
convictions on your verse?

VOICE

Our languages, including that
palaver we called dead, turns out to have
a longer memory than anyone alive.

The being born is passive
but the dying's active.
So one harbors

one's suspicion
that to die's ally must be
to bear. And as for being born,

or borne again, by God, it's not
a wish one ought
to want fulfilled, since there

the destiny's
not just the being dead.
It is the being killed.

DEAR GOD, HOW DO I FEEL?

After my friend was dead,
he took from in a closet, in a house
inside a dream, the presents

he had wrapped for everyone he loved. And I was there
to read the names, and pass the parcels on, till all
the gifts were given out. The closet finally

looked bare. I looked in there
for anything, or anyone, for him, for me
(come out! come out!)— but even we

had disappeared.

*

The most extreme
humility has its

own hubris. Brothers! Fathers!
Time itself the prized

presumption. Dressed
by Eddie Bauer, tramping far

and near, across the bog—Rex!
Rex! Come here, now, boy!—

the prince
entreats the dog.

A MISS IN THE MESS HALL

I can stick a shift
or rock a muu-muu.
You don't do me favors, mister;
I do you.

You needn't be my cat's paw.
Purr will do.
Make these become
the good old days.

We girls remember
how to gush: You're oh so neat,
my dearest! Be
my heart-throb! Seize me

now (one hand o'erturned
upon on her brow)! Back then
"my dearest" meant "my most expensive" and
the good old boys turned out

regrettable. Give them a shot,
they'd want the whole damn draft.
Arrests were getting
uniformly cardiac. Same strokes

for everyfolks! Good luck with that. Today we're all in
Eldercare. The milk
is spilt, the maids clean up. But there aren't any
messers anywhere.

MUSE ABUSE IN THE INDUSTRY

Terpsichore, your name
is known by every gigolo and jerk
in civilized society

to have four syllables. But when
the communes and the capitals alike
begin to go berserk,

economizing on the arts
of time and love, they start
to sell four syllables as three.

And that could turn your singing into work.

THE SPRING

One and the same
don't quite add up,
though one and one can still

requite. And yet the two
together play a minor part in all
the turmoil of a social life.

Over and over, head
and heel, two couples daily
miss the boat

because they dally. How to account
for dalliance? Or understand
the being prone? Take fall

and fall: A one-night
stand will never end
this free-for-all.

ON HIGH

There on the wing-tip, in the fog, is just
one light. Too late, the sign

of socked-in sensibility: It seems there is no end
of that closed mind, till suddenly

we're snapped right out of it, into another
world, a merciless

black clarity, a million miles of open, with a
twist of stars, a ping of lime!

*

In retrospect that little strife,
the mere extent of that
one smidgeon of

self-consciousness,
that blindest patch of mist about
a planet (not above a groundlessness)

turned out to be
the only place where we'd kick back
(without a lick of irony) and boast

This is the life!

NEVER GOTTEN OVER

in abiding honor of two irreplaceable friends: Elliot Fishbein and Raya Garbousova

Though she asked us outright, "Am I
dying?" no one said

"You are." Who hasn't lied about
unspeakabilities? Not I, to say

the least. Reflecting on
the surface stories, soon enough

we'd slide the Disney glitter she had been reduced to
overboard, across a gunnel

into deep and fast-revolving
irretrievabilities;

we let her go off five
whirlpools of island, hand to

reddened hand. The moon for once
appeared unmanned. But dolphins

wove some bubbles through
her vortices of spark. And all the while

our long hewn sides of lapstrake turned
into the whirlpool's play.

Some speak but cannot know.
Some know but cannot say.

ACKNOWLEDGMENTS

Several poems in this collection first appeared in the
following places: *Post Road Magazine, Hudson Review,
Swananoa Review* and at heathermchugh.com. Suzanna
Tamminen did yeoman's service putting up with vagaries
of stroke-struck brain when I was registering revisions.

HEATHER MCHUGH is the author of thirteen
previously published volumes of poetry, essays, and
translation (one a Pulitzer prize finalist and another
designated Book of the Year by *Publishers Weekly*). She
won a MacArthur "genius" Award in 2001, and used the
proceeds to fund restorative getaways for unpaid family
caregivers of people unable to walk, talk, or feed
themselves. *IT LOOKS LIKE A MAN* presents the voices of
characters attempting to understand, if not to love, the
changing surfaces and depths of worlds in which they find
themselves.

Wesleyan Chapbooks

Entanglements by Rae Armantrout

Notice by Rae Armantrout

A Las Orillas del Rio Viejo edited by Katherine Duarte

The Poetry Witch Little Book of Spells by Annie Finch

I Will Teach You About Murder: 29 Love Poems edited by
Shea Fitzpatrick, Sallie Fullerton, and Torii Johnson

*I Said That Love Heals from the Inside:
Love Poems of Yusef Komunyakaa* edited by Oliver Egger

I Ask My Mother to Sing: Mother Poems of Li-Young Lee
edited by Oliver Egger

Deaths of the Poets by Kit Reed, Illustrated by Joseph W. Reed

Dog Truths by Kit Reed, Illustrated by Joseph W. Reed

Thirty Polite Things to Say by Kit Reed, Illustrated by Joseph W. Reed